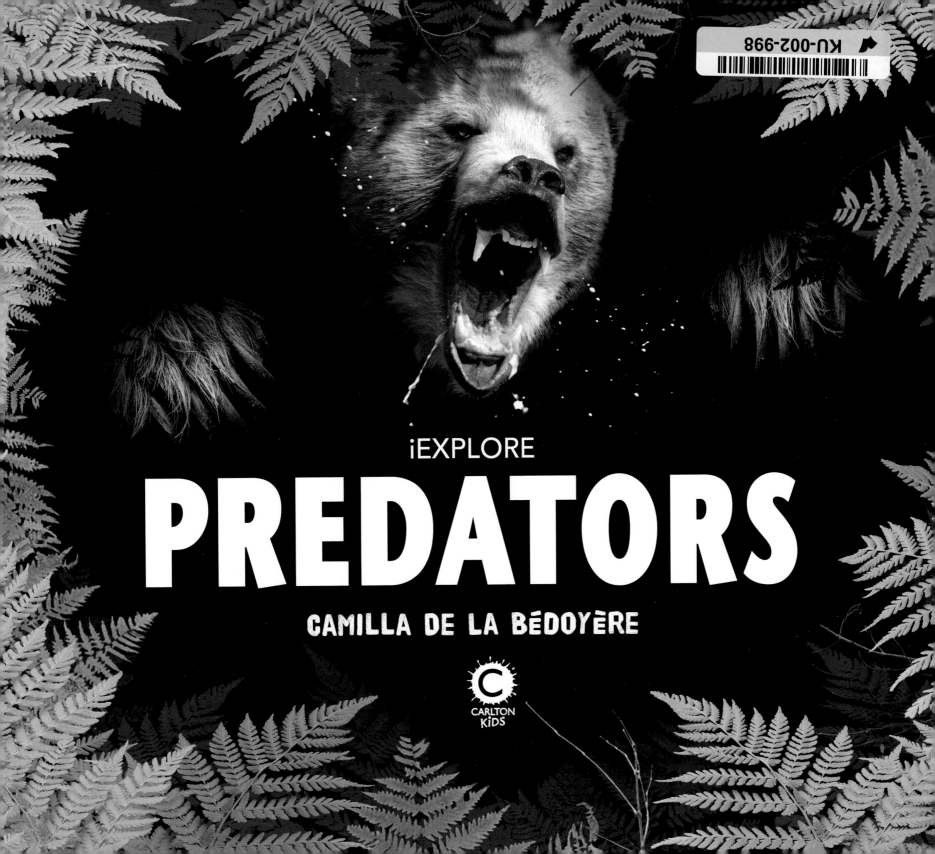

iEXPLORE

PREDATORS

CAMILLA DE LA BÉDOYÈRE

CARLTON
KiDS

BEWARE: PREDATORS

Life is a dangerous adventure for most animals. It's a battle for survival and sometimes only the strongest, meanest or smartest animals can win.

WHAT MAKES A PREDATOR?

A predator hunts and kills other animals, or prey, to eat. Most of the top predators have a selection of deady features that help them. Here are some of their key killer attributes:

1 CLAWS, JAWS AND TEETH

These weapons work like knives to grab, smash, slice and pierce a prey's body.

2 INTELLIGENCE

This invisible weapon makes the other ones far more effective. Some predators, such as orcas and lions, are smart enough to work as a group. This means they can plan attacks, and hunt animals bigger than themselves.

3

VENOM

A venomous bite gives some predators, such as the Komodo dragon, all the weaponry they need. Venom is a poison that can stop prey in its tracks, turning it into an almost lifeless zombie so a predator can enjoy its feast.

4

DEADLY SENSES

A top predator is likely to have super senses of sight, hearing and smell. Some predators, such as sharks and snakes, have extra powers that we can barely imagine.

LATIN NAME Panthera tigris

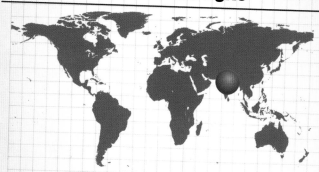

LOCATION Forests of southern and eastern Asia

SIZE

Up to 280 cm long

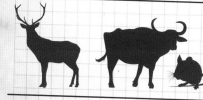

MAIN PREY
Deer, cattle, bears, small mammals and birds

BIG BITE
The famous tiger of Champawat holds the record for killing the most humans – more than 400 – before she was finally killed in 1907.

BALD EAGLE

One of the most majestic of all birds, a mighty bald eagle soars on warm air currents, high above the ground. As it flies, it searches the landscape below – and spots its next meal.

BIRDS OF PREY

The bald eagle belongs to a group of predators called birds of prey. They are large birds with incredible eyesight and the deadly claws and large beak that are needed to kill their prey. Birds of prey usually hunt in the daytime, except for owls, which are mostly nocturnal.

PERFECT FOCUS

An eagle has a great eye for detail. It can focus on a moving animal, such as a rabbit, from up to 2 kilometres away. It also has strength on its side: one bald eagle was seen carrying a deer in its talons!

TALONS AND TALENTS

Most birds of prey grab their prey with massive clawed feet, called talons. Some raptors are such superb hunters they can catch and kill birds while they are still in flight. Others – including bald eagles – are so skilled they can spy, swoop and grab slippery fish right out of water.

PREDATOR
ACTIVATION PAGE

INTERACT WITH A BALD EAGLE!

FAST FACTS

LATIN NAME Haliaeetus leucocephalus

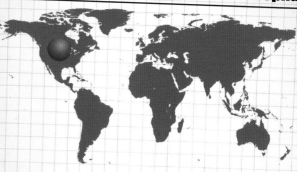

LOCATION
Forests, especially near water, in North America

SIZE

Wingspan up to 250 cm

MAIN PREY
Fish, ducks, rabbits and other small mammals

BIG BITE
An eagle's talon is smaller than a human hand, but it is about 10 times stronger, which means it can grip, rip and crush flesh.

RATTLESNAKE

Hunting in a grassy field, a rattlesnake senses the presence of another animal. It prepares to strike and, in a split-second, lunges with open jaws and venomous fangs.

VICIOUS VIPERS

Rattlesnakes belong to a group of snakes called vipers. Their long, slender fangs are hinged so they can be folded up into the snake's mouth. Some vipers lay eggs, but rattlesnakes give birth to up to 20 baby snakes at a time.

HEAT DETECTORS

A rattlesnake, like other pit vipers, can build up a picture of its prey using special senses. It has heat-sensitive pits between its nostrils and its eyes, and uses these to detect the warmth of another animal's body. It also flicks its tongue to taste the air and smell, and its long, sensitive body can feel the vibrations made by its prey moving nearby.

INSTANT DEATH

A rattlesnake bites its prey and, in just half a second, venom flows through its hollow fangs and into the victim's flesh, where it gets to work immediately. The snake can control how much venom it pumps into a victim so it delivers just the right amount for a quick death. A rattlesnake only needs to eat every 2 to 3 weeks.

PREDATOR
ACTIVATION PAGE

SEE A RATTLESNAKE STRIKE OUT TOWARDS YOU IN LIFESIZE!

FAST FACTS

LATIN NAME Crotalus atrox

North America

LOCATION
Hot, dry places in North America

SIZE

Up to 200 cm long

MAIN PREY
Birds and small mammals

BIG BITE
Snakes can open their jaws so wide they can swallow their prey whole. They can even eat animals bigger than themselves!

GREY WOLF

The spine-chilling howl of a wolf echoes eerily through the freezing winter air. The wolf is calling to its pack, telling the other wolves to come running. It's time to hunt...

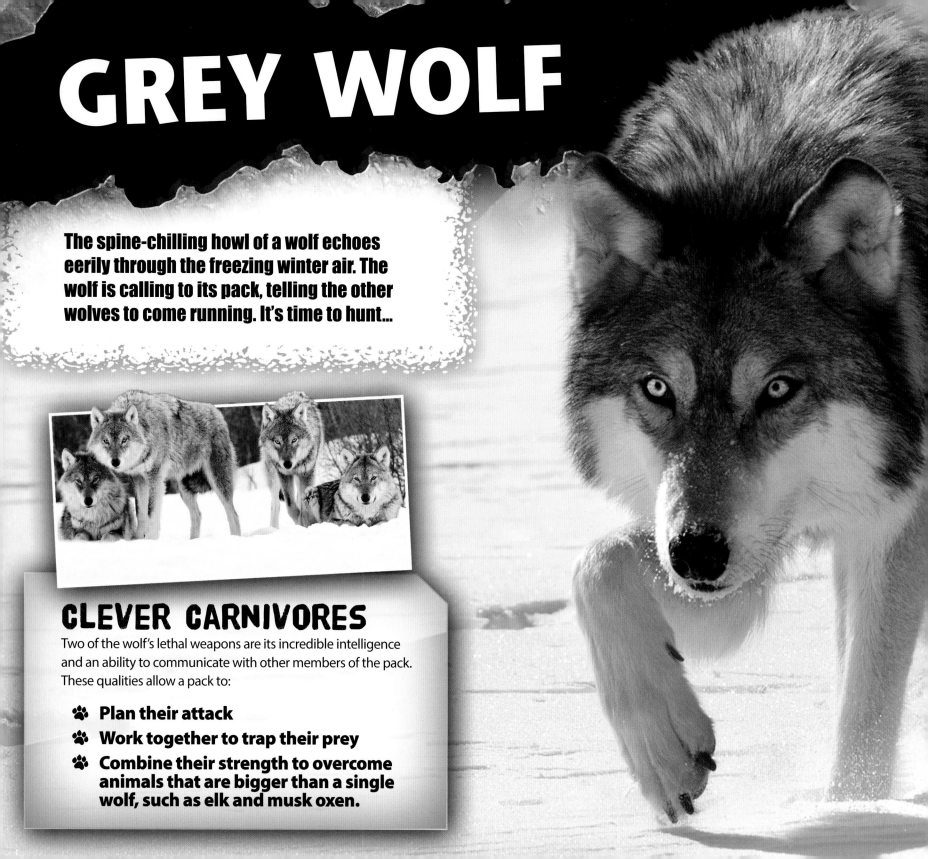

CLEVER CARNIVORES

Two of the wolf's lethal weapons are its incredible intelligence and an ability to communicate with other members of the pack. These qualities allow a pack to:

- 🐾 **Plan their attack**
- 🐾 **Work together to trap their prey**
- 🐾 **Combine their strength to overcome animals that are bigger than a single wolf, such as elk and musk oxen.**

ALPHA WOLVES

It is only the top male and female – the alpha pair – of the pack that can have cubs. The other group members always follow their lead and even help to raise and protect the youngsters.

CALL TO ACTION

The hunt begins when a wolf sees, smells or hears prey, and calls the rest of the pack. Together, they begin the chase, reaching speeds of up to 70 kilometres per hour. Wolves need to be fast to keep up with their favourite prey of swift-running deer. They have incredible stamina and can keep up a chase over great distances.

PREDATOR
ACTIVATION PAGE

SEE A GREY WOLF SNARL AND BARK AS YOU INTERACT WITH IT!

FAST FACTS

LATIN NAME Canis lupus

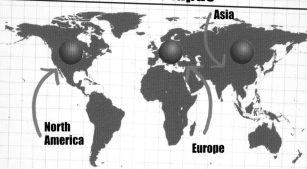

Asia

North America

Europe

LOCATION Cool northern forests of Europe, Asia and North America

SIZE

Up to 150 cm long

MAIN PREY
Deer and small mammals

BIG BITE
A wolf can eat up to 9 kilograms of meat in one go, shearing the flesh with its sharp, scissor-like teeth.

GREAT WHITE SHARK

A sleek, silent predator slips through the water, its black, cold eyes hinting at this beast's fearsome nature. This is one of the world's most awesome animals.

SUPER SENSES

The ocean is vast, so sharks need special skills to find their prey. They have an extraordinary sense of smell for detecting tiny traces of chemicals in water and they can smell blood and other body fluids from far away. Sharks also have an electric sense. They can detect the small amounts of electricity that are made in another animal's muscles.

DEADLY SPEED

When it's time to feed, a great white shark chases or ambushes its prey, approaching it from below with speeds of up to 40 kilometres per hour. It rams the victim, delivering a killer bite or a knockout blow from its large snout. Humans have little to fear from these sharks. It's extremely rare for humans to be attacked because great whites hunt seals and fish – and probably only hurt humans when they mistake them for their natural prey.

PREDATOR
ACTIVATION PAGE

DIVE UNDERWATER TO WATCH A LIFESIZE GREAT WHITE SWIM TOWARDS YOU.

NEW TEETH

Great white sharks, like most sharks, have rows of large teeth in their jaws. As teeth get damaged or fall out, the teeth in the row behind move forward to fill the gap. Each tooth can be more than 7 centimetres long and its edges are lined with serrations that help it 'saw' through tough skin and bones.

FAST FACTS

LATIN NAME Carcharodon carcharias

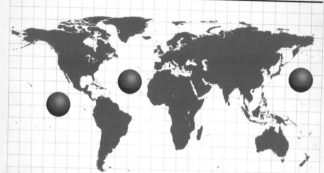

LOCATION Cool ocean waters, worldwide

SIZE

Up to 600 cm long

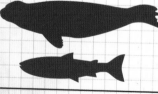

MAIN PREY
Fish and marine mammals

BIG BITE
A great white can have more than 400 teeth in its mouth, and it can get through 30,000 teeth in its lifetime!

LION

As the sun begins to set over the African plain, a lioness stirs herself from rest and prepares for the busy night ahead. These deadly cats prefer the cover of darkness for their hunting expeditions.

SECRETS OF SuCCESS

Lions judge distance very well and can see their prey even on dark, moonless nights. They have a special layer at the back of their eyes that reflects light, which is why cats' eyes appear to shine at night. Most big cats hunt alone, but lions live in family groups called prides. The lionesses are the pride's hunters and bring food home for the males and cubs.

KILLER SKILLS

During a hunt, a single lioness chases the prey, forcing it towards other lionesses who are lying in wait. They kill a big animal by leaping on it together. They dig their long, sharp claws into the prey and pull it down to the ground quickly. They have to act fast as a powerful kick from some animals, such as an antelope, could kill a lion.

FANGS

A lion's fangs can pierce through tough skin and their sharp, pointed teeth work like scissors to shear flesh. Lions cannot move their jaws from side to side, so they have to swallow large lumps of meat.

PREDATOR
ACTIVATION PAGE

FACE A FIERCE LIONESS IN LIFESIZE!

FAST FACTS

LATIN NAME Panthera leo

African grasslands

LOCATION African grasslands

SIZE

Up to 200 cm long

MAIN PREY
Zebras, antelope and other large mammals

BIG BITE
Lions and other big cats usually kill with a single bite to the throat, crushing the windpipe so the victim cannot breathe.

BROWN BEAR

The wintry sun shines down on the peaceful hillside. Suddenly, there's a crash and a roar as a brown bear appears – running at top speed, snarling and baring its teeth.

POWER TO KILL

This giant beast can stand more than 2 metres tall, but it runs on all fours, in huge leaping bounds. It attacks with a mighty punch from its front paws. Its strength and speed are so great that a single blow can kill an adult elk.

MOTHER LOVE

Although brown bears rarely attack humans for food, they will defend their families to the death. Mother bears are extremely protective of their cubs and will not hesitate to attack an animal, or a human, who threatens them.

BIG EATERS

Many predators are carnivores, which means they only eat meat. Brown bears, however, are omnivores: they eat a range of food including meat and plants, and use their 12-centimetre-long claws to dig. They particularly like berries, fruit, roots and shoots, but their diet can vary from seaweed to a baby deer! Some brown bears mostly feed on fish, which is such a healthy diet that they grow bigger and stronger than other bears. They stand in, or by, a river where salmon swim and leap out of the water and grab them with their claws or teeth.

PREDATOR
ACTIVATION PAGE

USE YOUR DEVICE TO
SEE A BROWN BEAR
STAND 2 METRES TALL!

FAST FACTS

LATIN NAME Ursus arctos

LOCATION Northern forests and grasslands of Europe, Asia and North America

SIZE

Up to 250 cm long

MAIN PREY
Mammals, birds, fish

BIG BITE
Brown bears can catch up to 30 fish a day. They gobble up the skin, brains and eggs but often throw the rest away!

ORCA

A big-brained beast leaps out of the water. It's part of a killing gang, and it is about to use its intelligence to plan and carry out a deadly attack on an unsuspecting victim.

KILLER WHALES

Orcas, or killer whales, live in family groups called pods. A hunting expedition begins with the 'spy hop', when orcas pop their heads out of water to look for seals resting on floating blocks of ice. Once a seal has been spotted, the orcas spread out. Several of them begin to swim towards the ice floe, creating a wave. The wave tips the ice, and the seal falls off… into the jaws of a waiting orca.

STUNNING HUNTERS

One technique for hunting strong prey, such as sea lions, is to find a weak, elderly or young victim, and separate it from its family. The orca chases it until the sea lion is exhausted or has run out of air. Orcas will also hit a shoal of fish with their tails, stunning the fish before eating them whole.

MOTHERS AND BABIES

Mothers teach their young how to hunt, even taking them to areas where there are plenty of baby grey whales to practise on. The young orcas attack the baby grey whales, while their mothers watch. If the youngsters fail to kill their prey the mothers join in and show them how it's done!

PREDATOR ACTIVATION PAGE

SEE A CUNNING ORCA UNDERWATER!

FAST FACTS

LATIN NAME Orcinus orca

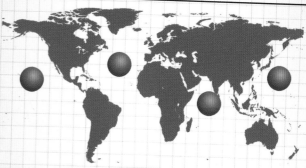

LOCATION Oceans worldwide

SIZE

Up to 900 cm long

MAIN PREY
Fish, squid, marine mammals

BIG BITE
An orca can reach top speeds of 56 kilometres per hour and leaps out of the sea, and on to ice to grab its prey.

SALTWATER CROCODILE

Though the river is calm, on its banks the master of ambush predators lies in wait. Combining stealth, speed and strength, this is one cool killer.

MONSTER REPTILES

Saltwater crocodiles, or salties, are fiercely aggressive and territorial. They are not fussy about who or what they attack – making them some of the most deadly animals on the planet and the largest animals that regularly prey on humans.

SUN, SEA AND SWIM

These are the world's largest reptiles, with an enormous pair of jaws. They lie near the water's edge, basking in the sun, or just under the water's surface. Saltwater crocodiles are superb swimmers. Their eyes and nostrils are on the top of their heads, which means they can see, breathe and smell as they swim.

SURPRISE ATTACK

When prey is spotted, a saltie turns on the speed and leaps forward to grab its victim in its teeth. Taken by surprise, the victim has no chance to escape or fight, and the crocodile pulls it beneath the water to drown it. A crocodile cannot chew, so it swallows its prey whole. If the prey is too large, the predator violently shakes its head from side to side, or spins round underwater to break it into smaller, bite-sized pieces.

PREDATOR ACTIVATION PAGE

WATCH A SALTIE LIE IN WAIT AND SUDDENLY ATTACK!

FAST FACTS

LATIN NAME Crocodylus porosus

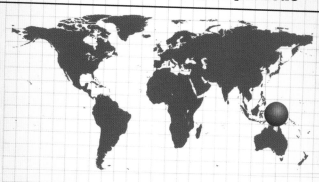

LOCATION Freshwater and seas around Southeast Asia and northern Australia

SIZE

Up to 600 cm long

MAIN PREY Mammals, reptiles, birds and fish

BIG BITE
A crocodile has 60 to 70 teeth that can pierce and rip flesh. It can eat half its body weight in one go!

KOMODO DRAGON

A lumbering giant reptile moves slowly across the dry scrubland of its island home. It flicks out its tongue, and senses the presence of a wild pig. Its killer instinct is switched on, and its stomach is empty.

SUPER-SIZED LIZARD

The Komodo dragon is the heaviest lizard in the world, weighing up to 70 kilograms in the wild. This great size gives it the strength it needs to tackle large prey, such as buffaloes. Komodo dragons are fearless and have been known to kill their own babies, as well as humans.

SCAVENGERS

Although Komodo dragons have good eyesight, they rely on their senses of smell and taste to find prey. Like snakes, they flick out their tongues to taste the air and detect the smell of a nearby animal. They are scavengers as well as predators, so they also use this sense to find carrion, animals that are already dead, which is an important part of their diet.

VILE VENOM

A Komodo dragon has the skills it needs to hunt, but it has a useful weapon for stopping any victim in its tracks: a deadly bite. Like some other reptiles, a Komodo dragon has venom in its spit. A Komodo dragon's venom sends its victims into shock and makes their wounds bleed so heavily that this alone can kill them.

PREDATOR
ACTIVATION PAGE

WATCH A KOMODO DRAGON MARCH TOWARDS YOU.

FAST FACTS

LATIN NAME Varanus komodoensis

LOCATION
Grasslands of Indonesian islands

SIZE

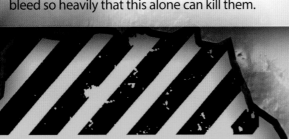

Up to 300 cm long

MAIN PREY
Buffaloes, wild pigs and deer

BIG BITE
A Komodo dragon can swallow a goat whole. Afterwards, it vomits up a lump of hooves, teeth, fur and horns.

SPOTTED HYENA

A blood-curdling 'whoop' is heard across the African grassland. It's the call of a spotted hyena, one of the world's fiercest, and most unusual, predators.

BIZARRE BEASTS

Hyenas are unusual because they look like dogs, but are more closely related to cats. They also live in large groups, called clans, that are ruled by the females, which are bigger and more aggressive than males. In fact, hyenas are so bold they will attack a pride of lions gorging on a feast of meat. They are tireless, refusing to give up, even in the face of several roaring, angry lions. It's not unusual for lions to skulk off, and leave their kill to the victorious hyenas!

PREDATOR ACTIVATION PAGE

WATCH A SPOTTED HYENA WALK AROUND YOUR ROOM!

MUNCH AND CRUNCH

A hyena's jaws are the strongest of any mammal of a similar size. Hyenas bite with such force they can even crunch through bone. Hyenas eat almost every part of an animal, leaving just the hard parts they cannot digest.

LAUGHING HYENAS

Hyenas are famous for their 'laugh'. This strange giggling sound is one of the many calls that hyenas use to communicate with each other, including groans and squeals. They 'laugh' when they are agitated or to tell another hyena that they want to be friends, not enemies.

FAST FACTS

LATIN NAME Crocuta crocuta

Grasslands of Africa

LOCATION
Grasslands of Africa

SIZE
Up to 130 cm long

MAIN PREY
Zebra, wildebeest, small mammals and birds

BIG BITE
Working together, a clan can attack big beasts, including young rhinos and buffaloes. They also attack humans.

POLAR BEAR

With long fangs and clawed paws, a polar bear can fight a rival to the death. At meal times, it puts those lethal weapons to work in another way: it can grab and kill a seal in seconds.

ICE AND SNOW

It's cold, bleak and almost always winter in the far north where polar bears live. The Arctic Ocean freezes, creating a massive sheet of ice that's covered in snow. In a place where plants can't grow, few animals can survive here.

FEAST OR FAMINE

Polar bears live lives of feast or famine because there is often plenty of food in summer, but they have to survive long periods without a meal in winter. They can do this because they have layers of blubber under their fur. During the worst weather, bears dig dens in the snow, and sleep. Cubs are born in these dens, and only emerge in the spring when there is more food around.

SNACK ATTACK

A polar bear's favourite prey is the ringed seal. These marine mammals breathe air, so they make 10-15 holes in the ice where they can emerge between fishing trips. That gives a bear the perfect opportunity to grab a snack.

PREDATOR
ACTIVATION PAGE

TAKE A PICTURE NEXT TO A HUGE POLAR BEAR!

FAST FACTS

LATIN NAME Ursus maritimus

LOCATION
Arctic Ocean and northern Canada

SIZE

Up to 340 cm long

MAIN PREY
Sea mammals, fish and caribou

BIG BITE
The polar bear is the world's largest land carnivore. It is big enough to kill small whales, and polar bears have been known to attack people.

MORE PREDATOR FACTS

The most dangerous sharks to humans are **BuLL SHARKS** and **TIGER SHARKS** because they live in warm coastal places, where people swim, wash and fish.

SAILFISH pursue shoals of fish at more than 100 kilometres per hour – that's faster than a cheetah can run.

The largest predator to ever live is the magnificent **BLUE WHALE**, with an average length of 25 metres. Despite their great size, these animals prey on tiny krill – shrimp-like animals that are no bigger than a finger!

The largest **NILE CROCODILE** ever seen is named Gustave, and he's rumoured to have killed more than 300 people. Gustave is said to be at least 6 metres long and 50 years old – but no one knows if he is still alive.

One of the most unusual predators is the little **VAMPIRE BAT**. It feeds on the blood of mammals or birds, using a heat sensor on its nose to find its victims.

PIRANHA FISH are amongst the most aggressive fish in the world, and are well equipped with jaws of razor-sharp teeth. They live in South American rivers and sometimes group together to devour larger animals in furious feeding frenzies.

One of the fastest-acting predators on Earth is the little **PEACOCK MANTIS SHRIMP**. It can punch its prey with the same force as a bullet – that's enough power to smash thick glass, and it's one of the speediest movements in nature.

THE BLACK MAMBA is one of the most feared snakes in Africa – its lethal bites inflict enough venom to kill 40 people!